Contents

Introducing the Rice Cooker

Why use a rice cooker?
- Rice cookers are simple and convenient to use, and are also inexpensive.
- Amazingly versatile and durable, rice cookers not only cook food but keep it warm and effectively reheat leftovers.
- They are safe to turn on and set to cook without the risk of burning food.
- Foods cooked in a rice cooker retain their nutrients.
- Cooking in a rice cooker is almost as fast as using a microwave, but, unlike the microwave, the rice cooker does not cook unevenly and therefore does not create cold spots in the food.

What can be cooked in a rice cooker?
Almost anything. You may be surprised at how many foods in addition to rice and whole grains can be cooked in a rice cooker, from soups, stews and pasta to vegetables, eggs and desserts.

How does a rice cooker work?
There are different types of rice cookers, but the most popular is the electric rice cooker. Often made of stainless steel, it consists of a rice cooker chamber with a spring loaded heating element at the bottom. A removable metal bowl, often non-stick and sometimes fitted with handles, sits in the rice cooker on the heating plate. Bowls with a nonstick surface are best, but if the surface is not nonstick, spray it with vegetable oil cooking spray before using. A lid seals the rice cooker. Some models have a metal or glass lid, others a vacuum-sealed lid and still others a locking lid that seals the cooker and keeps the rice moist (see picture page 6). The amount of liquid used in an electric rice cooker, including for rice, is usually less than the amount used in a pot on the stove top, as the lid seals the cooker, resulting in less evaporation.

Most electric rice cookers have "cook" and "warm" buttons. The cooker is designed to boil water fast when the "cook" button is pushed, then automatically reduce the heat as the heating element senses the water is absorbed and the rice is cooked. The cooker switches to "warm" and can hold food safely at 140°F (60°C) without burning it, from five to twelve hours, depending on the manufacturer.

The capacity of rice cookers is measured by the "rice cup," which is smaller than a conventional measuring cup. Usually, domestic models hold a range of 2 to 10 rice cups of uncooked rice. Rice cookers are sold with a rice cup. The inside of the rice cooker bowl is marked with measurements that correlate with the capacity of the rice cup. The proportion of water to rice is important, so be sure to use the same measuring cup for both rice and water.

Types of Rice Cookers

Simple rice cookers

- Usually the least expensive type, this electric on/off unit cooks rice, then turns off automatically. It does not have a light that indicates when the rice is cooked. The rice cooker bowl is usually not nonstick, and steamer racks are often not included.
- Cook and keep warm. Once the rice has cooked, the electric cooker reduces the heat automatically and keeps the rice warm for a period of time that varies from machine to machine, usually 5 to 12 hours. Nonstick pans and one, and sometimes two, steamer trays or racks may be included.

Fuzzy logic rice cookers

- Basic. The term "fuzzy logic" refers to microchip technology that makes a cooker more sophisticated, albeit more expensive. An electronic menu offers specific settings for different rice varieties. Some models include a slow-cook cycle for soups and stews, a reheat function that warms the rice in 5–10 minutes and maintains the heat, a quick-cook function that bypasses the rice soak time, a setting for choosing the preferred rice texture, from soft to firm, and a timer for presetting cooking times up to 24 hours ahead (see picture below).

On/off electric rice cooker with metal non-locking lid

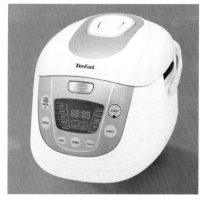

Microchip "fuzzy logic" rice cooker with vacuum-sealed locked lid

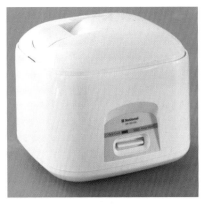

Vacuum-sealed electric rice cooker

Microwave rice cooker

■ Induction heating. This state-of-the-art, yet more expensive rice cooker can determine cooking times for different types of rice and food and can even compensate for measuring errors to produce perfectly cooked rice. A powerful magnetic field is created, so cooking starts immediately, even in the center of the food, resulting in fast, even cooking.

Microwave rice cookers

An inexpensive option, this cooker consists of a plastic bowl that is safe to use in a microwave as well as clean in a dishwasher. The bowl has a tight-fitting lid. This type is not usually intended for cooking large quantities. To use this cooker, cook on high for 5 minutes, then reduce to medium for 12–15 minutes for white rice and 35–45 minutes for brown. Then stand 5 minutes, covered.

Rice pots

This large, metal stove-top pot often has a nonstick surface for easy cleaning. It should have a tight-fitting metal or glass lid, and some come with steamer basket inserts. Buy good quality, or the heat tends to be uneven. There are also claypot rice cookers (see picture on right). As neither has the automatic cook and keep warm functions of the electric rice cookers, you need to monitor the cooking time.

Claypot rice cooker

Rice cooker accessories

Some are included with the cookers; others are optional.

RICE CUP This plastic cup, supplied with the rice cooker holds 4½–5 ounces (140–150 g) of uncooked rice and 5½ fluid ounces (165 ml) of water if filled to the water level marked on the cup or 6 fluid ounces (180 ml) if filled to the brim. The inside of the rice cooker bowl has marks that correlate to the capacity of the rice cup. If you misplace the cup, use a standard measuring cup (1 cup/250 ml) for both the rice and the water, following the cooking guide on page 19. When you use a standard cup, recipes may need to be adjusted accordingly. The recipes in this book use a standard measuring cup for rice and liquid, not a rice cup.

STEAMER TRAYS Some rice cookers are designed to accommodate one or two trays, racks or baskets for steaming foods, especially vegetables. As these foods steam in the tray, rice, pasta or more vegetables can be cooked underneath it.

RETRACTABLE OR REMOVABLE CORD The power cord on some models retracts into the appliance and the cord on others can be removed. This feature is an advantage when storing the cooker and when bringing it from the kitchen to the table for serving.

CARRY HANDLE A handle is useful for taking the cooker to the table for serving.

RICE PADDLE/SPATULA This plastic or wooden paddle or spatula is for fluffing cooked rice and for serving it. Metal utensils should not be used as they can scratch the nonstick surface of the rice cooker bowl. Some models have a spatula holder that attaches to the side of the cooker.

PLASTIC TONGS Tongs made of plastic or coated in plastic are preferred over metal as they do not scratch the nonstick surface of the rice cooker bowl.

COLANDER/STRAINER A colander or strainer is useful for draining rice. It should have fine mesh so the grains do not fall through the grid.

Care and cleaning

- A nonstick surface on the rice cooker bowl ensures easy cleaning.
- Use a plastic or wooden rice paddle and plastic tongs, not metal utensils, to avoid scratching the nonstick surface.
- Before starting to cook, clean the underside of the rice cooker bowl and the surface of the heating plate.
- After using the rice cooker, remove the bowl and wash in hot, soapy water, then rinse and dry completely before returning to the rice cooker.
- If rice has stuck to the bottom of the bowl, fill it with hot, soapy water and let stand for 10 minutes before cleaning.
- Some rice cookers have a detachable lid for easy cleaning. Others have a spoon holder and a condensation cup that attach to the side of the cooker. Remove both attachments, empty any liquid from the cup, then wash and dry the items.
- Using a dry, clean kitchen towel, wipe any condensation from around the inner seal of the lid if it has one (some rice cookers have a lid without a seal).

Troubleshooting

- If the cooker is not working properly, check the rice cooker bowl. It must be properly positioned inside the cooker. To ensure that the bowl is sitting flat on the heating plate, rotate it a few times.
- If the cook button will not stay on in "cook" position when heating the oil to brown ingredients before cooking, activate the spring loaded heating element.
- If "cook" button turns off before food is browned sufficiently, simply switch it on again. If it still will not stay in "on" position, wait a few minutes and try again.

Steaming foods in a rice cooker

The advantage of steaming foods is that they generally do not require the use of oil and retain most of their nutritional value. Some rice cookers are designed with one or two steamer trays. Food can be placed in the tray above the stock or water, the lid closed and the cooker turned on. If no trays are supplied, a trivet can be put in the bottom of the rice cooker bowl, and the food can be placed on a heatproof plate or bowl and set on the trivet.

Be sure that the steamer tray or trivet does not touch the liquid in the rice cooker bowl. A plate or bowl used with a trivet must allow steam to circulate evenly. Finally, do not let the liquid in the rice cooker bowl boil dry. Liquid can be added during the steaming process, if required; be sure to add hot liquid in order to maintain the proper temperature.

Tips

- Cut foods into uniform sizes for even cooking.
- Smaller pieces steam faster than larger ones.
- Slower-cooking vegetables can be added earlier or cut into smaller pieces than faster-cooking vegetables, for more even cooking.
- Vegetables can be cooked longer than usual if a soft texture is desired. More water should be added to the rice cooker if needed.
- Frozen vegetables do not need to be defrosted before steaming.
- Food should be arranged in a single layer for even cooking.
- As steamed food can look bland, sear meat and poultry before steaming, if desired.
- Place parchment (baking) paper or cabbage or lettuce leaves under dumplings to prevent them from sticking to the steamer tray.
- Seafood and chicken can be wrapped in parchment (baking) paper (see picture below left), aluminum foil or blanched leaves, such as banana or bamboo. Cooking food in parcels not only contains the juices, which can be served as a sauce, but also allows individual servings to be seasoned to taste. The parcels are also attractive to serve to guests.
- Timing is based on the thickness of food, not on the weight.
- Do not put the food to be steamed over the liquid until the liquid is simmering. Cooking time starts then.

Steaming cooking guide

A number of variables affect cooking times when steaming food in a rice cooker. Among them are the size and thickness of food and the amount being cooked, whether the steamer is close to or far above the simmering liquid, and whether one or two steamers are used. Since cooking times can vary, always check food after the shortest cooking time. Cooking time for vegetables will depend on preferred crispness.

Seafood
- Fish fillets: 5–8 minutes (depending on thickness and texture)
- Fish steaks: 8–12 minutes (depending on thickness)
- Mussels, in shell: 5–10 minutes
- Clams, in shell: 4–8 minutes
- Shrimp: 4–6 minutes (depending on size)
- Scallops: 3–4 minutes
- Lobster tails: 12–15 minutes

Chicken
- Breast halves, boneless: 12–15 minutes
- Thighs, boneless: 15–18 minutes
- Drumsticks, bone in: 20–25 minutes

Vegetables
- Asparagus spears: 3–5 minutes
- Beans, green: 5–7 minutes
- Beets, small whole (3 oz/90 g): 15–20 minutes
- Broccoli, florets: 5–8 minutes
- Carrots, thin slices: 5–8 minutes
- Potatoes, medium whole (6 oz/ 180 g): 30–35 minutes
- Potatoes, whole new (4 oz/125 g): 20–25 minutes
- Sweet potatoes (kumeras) (2-in/5-cm chunks): 15–20 minutes
- Winter squash (pumpkin) (2-in/5-cm chunks): 15–20 minutes
- Zucchini (courgette), sliced: 5 minutes

List of **Ingredients**

Basil is used as a seasoning and garnish in many Asian cuisines. Thai basil *(horapa)* tastes rather like Italian sweet basil but with an added hint of anise and is used in red and green curries as well as salads and stir-fries. It is available year round. If you cannot find it, use Italian basil.

Bell Peppers, also known as capsicums, have a crunchy texture and a fresh, tangy taste. The most popular peppers are green and red, but sweeter yellow and orange peppers have become more widely available.

Cardamom pods are highly aromatic and contain tiny black seeds. If whole pods are used, they should be removed from the food before serving. If only the seeds are called for, lightly smash the pods and remove the seeds, discarding the pods. Ground cardamom is sold in packets or tins.

Dried chilies

Bird's-eye chilies

Finger-length chilies

Chili peppers come in many shapes, sizes and colors. Fresh green and red Asian **finger-length chilies** are moderately hot. **Dried chilies** are usually deseeded, cut into lengths and soaked in warm water to soften before use. **Chili sauce** is made by mixing ground chilies with water and seasoning the mixture with salt, sugar and vinegar or lime juice. It is available bottled and in jars.

Chinese five spice powder is a ground spice mixture consisting of star anise, fennel, cloves, cinnamon and pepper. An ingredient mainly used in Chinese cooking, it is sold in small plastic packets or jars in Chinese grocery stores or the spice section of supermarkets.

Cinnamon is lighter in color, thinner, and more expensive than cassia bark, which is often sold as cinnamon. Cassia bark has a stronger flavor than cinnamon, but makes an acceptable substitute. Do not use ground cinnamon as a substitute where cinnamon sticks are called for.

Cloves are native to the Moluccan islands of Indonesia, though they have been grown in India for centuries. Use the whole, dark brown nail-shaped spice rather than ground cloves. Store in an airtight container away from light.

Thick **coconut cream** is thick, rich liquid squeezed from shredded coconut that has been soaked in water. Available in cans or packets from most stores. Keep refrigerated once open and use within 3–4 days, or freeze. Thin coconut cream is also known as **coconut milk**. This is extracted from shredded coconut soaked in water for a second time after coconut cream is extracted. Keep refrigerated or freeze, as with coconut cream. Lite coconut milk, with lower fat content, is also available in Asian food stores.

Coriander leaves (also known as cilantro or Chinese parsley) are the pungent, fragrant leaves of the coriander plant. They have a fresh aroma and flavor and are used widely in Asian cuisines as a herb and as a garnish. Italian parsley or basil may be substituted, although the

flavor is not exactly the same. Small, round **coriander seeds** are slightly citrussy in fragrance and are used whole or ground in curry pastes and spice mixes.

Cumin seeds are pale brown to black in color and have thin ridges on the outside. They impart an earthy flavor and are used whole, or roasted and ground. Cumin seeds are usually partnered with coriander seeds in basic spice mixes, and are often dry-roasted or fried in oil to intensify their flavor. Cumin seeds are believed to aid digestion and are used in most Indian spice blends.

Dried black Chinese mushrooms are intensely flavorful mushrooms that are sold fresh or dried. They have a dark brown outer skin, a beige inner flesh and a slightly woody

flavor. The dried mushrooms need to be rehydrated before use. Soak in boiling water for 15 to 30 minutes and squeeze dry before slicing or chopping the caps; discard the tough stems.

Fennel, as a spice, refers to the dried seeds of the fennel plant, although the plant itself is used as both a herb and a vegetable. The spice is elongated with an oval almond shape and is greenish to yellowish-brown in color, looking very similar to cumin but larger and lighter in color. It has a very distinctive, sweet taste with an aroma of aniseed and lemon and a whiff of dill. Whole and ground fennel are sold in Asian markets. Substitute aniseed or cumin.

Garlic chives, also known as Chinese chives, have thin flat leaves that resemble thin green onions (scallions). They have a strong garlicky flavor and are added to noodle or stir-fried dishes during the final stages of cooking. If you cannot get them, use green onions or regular chives.

Green onions, also known as scallions or spring onions, have slender stalks with dark green leaves and white bases. They are sliced and sprinkled generously on soups and used as a garnish in Chinese cooking.

Hoisin sauce consists of fermented soybeans, sugar, garlic, chilies and vinegar. The sauce is thick and dark and has a sweet, salty flavor. Commercially bottled or canned hoisin sauce is available in many grocery stores.

Kaffir lime leaves have an unusual double green leaf on one stem with a very intense citrus flavor. Although available fresh, frozen or dried, nothing equals its unique and strong flavor when fresh. Use whole to infuse flavor, discarding before serving, or remove the hard stems and finely cut into very thin threads with scissors before use. Keep refrigerated. The juice and grated rind of the fruit are also used, but regular lime juice and rind can be substituted.

Lotus seeds are most commonly eaten in desserts. Most lotus seeds are sold with the bitter central core or endosperm already removed (if so, the seeds will have a narrow slit on both sides). Sometimes, there are a few rogues with the cores still intact, so check and if you see a dark greenish center at the top of the seed, split it open and flick out the core. Dried lotus seeds may be stored in an airtight container in the cupboard; they keep for many months.

Mint leaves are sold as fresh sprigs or dried and minced. Store fresh mint in the refrigerator, wrapped in paper towels and sealed in a plastic bag. Bottles of dried mint leaves should be stored away from light, heat and moisture. Just before use, crush the dried leaves in your palm to release their flavor.

Mirin is a sweet alcoholic wine made from rice and used in Japanese cooking. Sweet sherry may be substituted.

Paprika is a dried ground seasoning made from red bell pepper. There are several varieties of paprika—hot and smoked are the most popular ones. Paprika is used to add both color and flavor to dishes. The sweet variety is available in most supermarkets.

Rice vinegar is made from glutinous rice and has a mild, sour flavor. It is colorless and is one of the definitive ingredients used in sweet and sour sauce. Substitute mild white wine vinegar.

Saffron is originally from India and is known as the queen of spices. It is picked with near religious fervor before dawn, which explains its price. Be careful not to buy counterfeits which are sometimes made with silk from corn husks and a little oil. Saffron is always used in festive dishes. You can sub-

stitute ground turmeric though it has neither the sublety nor the strength.

Sesame seeds are commonly pan-roasted to bring out their nutty flavor before being added to dishes. You can buy them already roasted or raw and then roast them yourselves in a dry skillet, moving them around so that they turn golden brown and do not burn. Black sesame seeds have a slightly bitter flavor and are sometimes used for decoration.

Sesame oil is an amber-colored aromatic oil made from toasted sesame seeds. Used to add a nutty flavor to dishes at the end of cooking. Use sparingly as it is strong. Store in a cool, dark cupboard.

Star anise is a dried brown flower with 8 woody petals, each with a shiny seed inside, which

gives a flavor of cinnamon and aniseed. Use whole and remove from the dish before serving. It is available in plastic packets in the spice section of Asian markets and well-stocked supermarkets.

Turmeric is a root related to ginger, with a slightly bitter, pungent flavor and intense yellow-orange color. Used to add flavor and color to dishes. Available fresh and dried from stores. Refrigerate if fresh.

Wonton wrappers are small pliable square or round sheets of domade from flour, egg and salt, available in variothickness. Used to wrap savory and sweet fillings. Available refrigerated or frozen. Use refrigerated wrappers within 7 days of purchase.

Types of Rice

Brown rice and polished white rice are the two common types used in the kitchen. When brown rice is processed, only the inedible outer husk is removed. The nutritious, high-fiber bran coating is retained and gives the rice a light tan color, a chewy texture and a slightly nutty flavor. Because the bran is not removed, brown rice turns rancid more quickly and takes longer to cook than white rice. Instant or quick brown or white rice has been fully or partially parboiled, then dehydrated, and cooks in half or less the normal time, but tends to lack flavor and texture. The proportion of Amylopekin and amylose starch content determines the moisture of the rice amd therefore its cooking quantities.

Rice is classified by its size and shape:

LONG-GRAIN The grains, whether brown or white, are four or five times longer than they are wide, with higher amylose starch content. When cooked, they become light and dry and separate easily. This type of rice is ideal for pilafs and rice salads.

MEDIUM-GRAIN Shorter and moister than long grain rice, but not as starchy as short grain. The grains are fairly fluffy when cooked, but begin to clump once they start to cool. These properties make the rice suitable for desserts, paella and sushi and for eating with chopsticks.

SHORT-GRAIN Plump, almost round grains with a higher amylopectin starch content than long or medium grains. This type is ideal for making desserts and sushi and for eating with chopsticks.

Arborio rice

Basmati rice

Calasparra rice

Glutinous rice

Common varieties of rice

ARBORIO An Italian rice with short- to medium-grains and a high starch content that gives the cooked rice a creamy texture. The grains swell and absorb a greater amount of liquid than many other rice varieties. Used for risotto and other Mediterranean dishes. Carnaroli super fino, and the slightly smaller Vialone Nano semi fino, similar varieties, are especially well suited for making risotto. Unlike other rice, Arborio is not rinsed before cooking for dishes like risotto as the surface starch adds to the creaminess of the dish.

BASMATI A dry, aromatic, long-grain rice. It benefits from being soaked in water for 30 minutes before cooking or adding slightly more water when cooking. Suited to Indian and Middle Eastern dishes. Texmati is an American variety of basmati grown in Texas.

CALASPARRA A Spanish medium-grain rice, traditionally used for paella. Arborio can be substituted.

GLUTINOUS RICE Short-grain rice with a sticky texture, hence its alternative name, sticky rice. Used in Asian cooking, mainly in desserts and sweets such as Japanese mochi, and sometimes sushi. Soak before cooking.

JASMINE A subtly fragrant, soft, long-grain rice. Commonly used in Asian dishes, especially Thai and Vietnamese.

SUSHI Short or medium grain, and also sold as Nishiki or Koshihikari rice. It is moist and slightly sweet, so in Japan it is not traditionally cooked with salt. Because the cooked grains gently cling together, the rice can be eaten with chopsticks and molded for preparations such as sushi.

THAI BLACK RICE A long-grain rice with a chewy texture and grassy flavor well suited for use in desserts, especially those with coconut milk and fruit. This type benefits from being soaked overnight before cooking. The soluble bran coating leaches into the soaking and cooking liquid, coloring it purple.

Jasmine rice

Sushi rice

Thai black rice

Wild rice

Cooking Perfect Rice

Whether you use a standard measuring cup or a cooker's rice cup, the preparation for cooking rice is the same. Measure the rice and then rinse it according to the directions in individual recipes. If using a standard measuring cup, measure the water with the same cup. If using a rice cup, put the rice in the rice cooker bowl and add the water to the equivalent rice cup measure marked on the inside of the bowl. For example, if you measured 2 rice cups of rice, put the rice in the cooker, then add the water up to the 2 cup level on the bowl.

RINSING RICE Most rice varieties benefit from being rinsed in cold water until the water runs clear. This removes excess starch so the rice does not become sticky. The exceptions are Arborio and related types, as the starch on the surface of the grains contributes the appealing creaminess characteristic of dishes like risotto.

SOAKING THE RICE Although it's not essential, some rice varieties, such as basmati and brown rice, should be rinsed and then soaked in water for 30 minutes or more before cooking. Short- or medium-grain rice used for sushi also benefits from soaking, to help ensure uniform cooking and optimum texture.

Tips

- For measuring rice, use the rice cup provided with the rice cooker. Cups may vary with different brands of cookers (see cooking guide on opposite page).
- Always measure the rice by filling the cup level with the rim, or level marked on cup. Never use heaping cups.
- Because rice increases in volume as it cooks, never fill the rice cooker beyond its recommended capacity.
- Always cook the minimum quantity of rice recommended by the manufacturer, usually 2 rice cups.
- Once the rice is cooked, open the lid and turn the rice with a rice paddle. Close the lid and leave the rice undisturbed for 10–15 minutes to allow excess moisture to be absorbed. This will result in fluffier, more evenly cooked rice.
- For firmer rice, use slightly less water; for softer rice, add slightly more.
- Certain types of rice, such as Arborio and wild rice blends, may require more liquid than other varieties.
- When cooking large quantities of rice, the amount of water can be decreased slightly. The cooking time will need to be increased slightly (this will happen automatically, if using an electric cooker).
- Rice that is nearing its expiration date may require slightly more water than new-season rice as the grains have lost some of their moisture.

Cooking guide

Using standard measuring cup

Uncooked amount 1 cup (220 g) white rice
Water 1 cup (250 ml)
Yield About 3 cups (470 g)
Cooking Time 15 minutes

Uncooked amount 1 cup (220 g) brown rice
Water 1 cup (250 ml)
Yield About 2½ cups (375 g)
Cooking Time 35–40 minutes

Uncooked amount 1 cup (220 g) wild rice
Water 1 cup (250 ml)
Yield About 2½ cups (375 g)
Cooking Time 35–40 minutes

Using rice measuring cup

White rice
Uncooked amount 2 rice cups
Water 2 rice cups
Yield 4 rice cups
Cooking Time 15 minutes

Uncooked amount 4 rice cups
Water 4 rice cups
Yield 8 rice cups
Cooking Time 18 minutes

Uncooked amount 6 rice cups
Water 6 rice cups
Yield 12 rice cups
Cooking Time 22 minutes

Brown rice
Uncooked amount 2 rice cups
Water 3 rice cups
Yield 5 rice cups
Cooking Time 25–30 minutes

Uncooked amount 4 rice cups
Water 6 rice cups
Yield 10 rice cups
Cooking Time 35–40 minutes

Uncooked amount 6 rice cups
Water 9 rice cups
Yield 15 rice cups
Cooking Time 40–45 minutes

Reheating cooked rice

Put leftover cooked rice in the rice cooker bowl. Add 2–3 tablespoons water or stock, close the lid and activate the "cook" switch. Stir the rice occasionally, adding more water or stock if necessary, and cook until the rice is heated through. Push "warm" to keep the rice warm until serving.

Rice Dishes

WHITE RICE

1¹/₂ cups (315 g) uncooked
long- or short-grain
white rice
1¹/₂ cups (375 ml) water
¹/₂ teaspoon salt (optional)

SERVES 4
MAKES 4¹/₂ cups (690 g)

1 Put the rice in a bowl with enough cold water to cover. Gently rub the grains together with your fingers to remove any excess surface starch. Drain. Repeat 3 or 4 times until the water is nearly clear.
2 Combine the rice, water and salt (if using) in the rice cooker bowl, spreading the rice evenly in the bottom of the bowl. Close the lid and press "cook." Cook until the rice cooker turns to "warm," 12–15 minutes.
3 Fluff the rice with a rice paddle, close the lid and let stand for 10–15 minutes to absorb any remaining moisture.

BROWN RICE

2 cups (440 g) uncooked
brown rice
3 cups (750 ml) water or
stock
1 teaspoon salt (optional)

SERVES 4
MAKES 5 cups (780 g)

1 Put the rice in a bowl with enough cold water to cover. Gently rub the grains together with your fingers to remove any excess surface starch. Drain.
2 Combine the rice, water and salt (if using) in the rice cooker bowl, spreading the rice evenly in the bottom of the bowl. If time permits, let stand for 30 minutes before cooking. Close the lid and press "cook." Cook until the rice cooker turns to "warm," 35–40 minutes.
3 Fluff the rice with a rice paddle, close the lid and stand for 10–15 minutes to absorb any remaining moisture.

This recipe produces rice with a firm texture. For softer rice, add ¹/₄ –¹/₂ cup (60–125 ml) more water, depending on preferred texture.

EASY RECIPE VARIATIONS

Saffron rice Add 5–10 saffron threads for every 1 cup (250 ml) water.

Savory rice with herbs Substitute beef, chicken, fish or vegetable stock for water. Stir chopped fresh flat-leaf (Italian) parsley, dill, basil, chives or coriander leaves (cilantro) into the cooked rice.

Sweet rice For half of the water, substitute fruit juice. Using milk products is not recommended as they will scorch the bottom of the rice cooker bowl. Instead, stir cream or yogurt into the rice after it is cooked. Chopped fresh fruit may also be stirred into the hot cooked rice.

QUICK AND EASY RICE SALADS

Put the hot, cooked rice in a large, shallow dish to cool. This also helps keep the rice grains separate. Combine the warm cooked rice with salad dressing so the grains can absorb the flavor. Cover and refrigerate, then add one of the following combinations:

Cherry tomatoes, halved; English (hothouse) cucumber, sliced; red bell pepper, chopped; toasted pine nuts; fresh (flat-leaf) parsley, chopped; green onions (scallions), thinly sliced; strips of smoked chicken.

Sliced or bite-sized grilled vegetables such as zucchini (courgette), onion and red bell peppers; crumbled feta cheese; oil-packed sun-dried tomatoes, drained and cut into thin strips; black olives such as Niçoise or Kalamata.

Orange segments, cut in half; black olives such as Niçoise or Kalamata; thinly sliced onion; fennel bulb, trimmed and cut into thin strips; cooked shrimp.

Dried apricots, thinly sliced; toasted almonds or cashews; dried currants; toasted pumpkin seeds; toasted cumin seeds, crushed or left whole; chopped fresh mint; green onions (scallions), thinly sliced; grilled lamb tenderloin, thinly sliced.

INDIAN TOMATO RICE

1 cup (220 g) uncooked basmati rice
1 tablespoon oil
1 small onion, chopped
2 cloves garlic, finely chopped
1 red finger-length chili, deseeded and chopped
1 teaspoon cumin seeds
6 peppercorns
2 whole cloves
1 cinnamon stick
$^1/_2$ cup (75 g) fresh or frozen peas
1 cup (200 g) canned whole tomatoes
2 tablespoons tomato paste
$^1/_2$ teaspoon salt
$1^3/_4$ cups (440 ml) water or stock
2 tablespoons chopped fresh coriander leaves (cilantro)

1 Put the rice in a bowl with enough cold water to cover. Gently rub the grains together with your fingers to remove any excess surface starch. Drain. Return the rice to the bowl, add enough cold water to cover and let stand for 5 minutes. Drain and set aside.

2 Place the oil in the rice cooker bowl, press "cook" and heat for 1 minute. Add the onion, garlic and chili and cook, stirring constantly, until the onion is soft, about 2 minutes.

3 Add the cumin seeds, peppercorns, cloves and cinnamon stick and cook for 2 minutes. Stir in the rice, peas, tomatoes and tomato paste, and cook, stirring constantly, until well combined, about 2 minutes. Add the salt and water or stock.

4 Close the lid and cook until the rice cooker switches to "warm," 12–15 minutes. Stir with a rice paddle, close the lid and let stand for 10 minutes on "warm." Using a fork, stir in the coriander leaves. Remove the whole cloves and cinnamon stick before serving.

SERVES 4

INDIAN PILAF RICE

1¹/₄ cups (280 g) uncooked basmati rice
1 tablespoon oil
1 onion, chopped
2 cloves garlic, finely chopped
1 teaspoon fennel seeds
1 tablespoon sesame seeds
¹/₂ teaspoon ground turmeric
1 teaspoon ground cumin
¹/₂ teaspoon salt
2 whole cloves
3 cardamom pods, lightly crushed
6 peppercorns
1³/₄ cups (440 ml) chicken stock
Curry leaves, for garnish (optional)

1 Put the rice in a bowl with enough cold water to cover. Gently rub the grains together with your fingers to remove any excess surface starch. Drain. Return the rice to the bowl, add enough cold water to cover and let stand for 30 minutes. Drain and set aside.

2 Place the oil in the rice cooker bowl, press "cook" and heat for 1 minute. Add the onion and garlic and cook, stirring constantly, until the onion is soft, about 2 minutes. Stir in the fennel seeds, sesame seeds, turmeric, cumin, salt, cloves, cardamom and peppercorns. Cook, stirring constantly, until fragrant, 1–2 minutes.

3 Add the rice and cook, stirring constantly, until the grains are opaque, about 2 minutes. Pour in the stock. Close the lid and cook until the rice cooker switches to "warm," 12–15 minutes.

4 Stir with a rice paddle, close the lid and let stand for 10 minutes on "warm." Garnish with the curry leaves, if desired.

SERVES 4

EASY SUSHI RICE

1¹/₂ cups (315 g) uncooked short-grain or sushi rice such as Koshihikari or Nishiki, rinsed
1¹/₂ cups (375 ml) water
3 tablespoons rice vinegar
2 tablespoons sugar
³/₄ teaspoon salt

MAKES 6 cups (940 g)

1 Combine the rice and water in the rice cooker bowl, spreading the rice evenly in the bottom of the bowl.
2 Close the lid and press "cook." Cook until the cooker switches to "warm," 12–15 minutes. Stir the rice with a rice paddle, close the lid and let stand for 10 minutes on "warm." Transfer the rice to a large, shallow glass or ceramic dish.
3 Heat the vinegar, sugar and salt in a small saucepan over low heat until the sugar dissolves.
4 Pour the vinegar mixture over the rice and, holding a plastic or wooden rice spatula at a 45-degree angle, slice through the rice to break up any lumps and evenly distribute the vinegar mixture. Spread the rice out and let cool to room temperature. Cover with a damp kitchen towel to prevent the rice from drying out until ready to use.

SUSHI RICE WITH TOPPINGS

1 recipe Easy Sushi Rice (see above)
Toppings of your choice, such as thinly sliced somked salmon, sashimi tuna or salmon, sliced English (hothouse) cucumber and avocado, thin asparagus spears, blanched snowpeas
Wasabi paste, to serve
Slices of pink pickled ginger (gari), to serve
Japanse soy sauce, to serve

1 Prepare the Easy Sushi Rice by following the recipe above.
2 Divide the Easy Sushi Rice among 4 bowls. Arrange a selection of ingredients on the rice: Thinly sliced smoked salmon, sashimi tuna or salmon; sliced English (hothouse) cucumber and avocado; thin asparagus spears, blanched and sliced on the diagonal into 2-in (5-cm) pieces; blanched snowpeas (mange-tout).
3 Serve accompanied with wasabi, slices of pink pickled ginger (gari) and Japanese soy sauce.

SERVES 4

CLASSIC SEAFOOD PAELLA

2 tablespoons oil

1 onion, diced

2 cloves garlic, crushed

1 sausage, removed from casing and sliced

$1/2$ teaspoon smoked paprika or 1 teaspoon sweet or hot
   paprika

2 cups (440 g) uncooked Arborio or long-grain rice, rinsed

$3/4$ lb (375 g) skinless, boneless chicken thighs, cut into
   2-in (5-cm) pieces

1 can (440 g) canned whole tomatoes

3 cups (750 ml) chicken stock, plus more if needed

1 teaspoon salt

1 teaspoon saffron threads soaked in $1/4$ cup (60 ml) boiling
   water

$3/4$ lb (375 g) medium shrimp, peeled and deveined

8 mussels, scrubbed and debearded

About 8 oz (250 g) calamari, cleaned and thinly sliced, or 6 oz
   (180 g) calamari tubes, thinly sliced crosswise (optional)

1 red bell pepper, roasted (page 33), peeled, deseeded and
   thinly sliced

1 cup (150 g) fresh or frozen peas

1 lemon, cut into 6 wedges

1 Place the oil in the rice cooker bowl, press "cook"
and heat for 1 minute. Add the onion, garlic and
sausage and cook, stirring occasionally, until the onion
softens slightly, about 2 minutes.

2 Stir in the paprika and rice and cook, stirring constantly,
until the grains are opaque, about 2 minutes. Add the
chicken, tomatoes, stock, salt and saffron, and stir to combine. Close the lid and press "cook." Cook for 15 minutes.

3 Stir in the seafood, bell pepper and peas. Close the lid
and cook until the rice cooker switches to "warm,"
5–10 minutes. Add more stock or water if the rice
needs further cooking or if softer rice is desired.

4 Close the lid and let stand for 10 minutes or longer
if drier texture is desired. Serve with the lemon
wedges scattered on top.

SERVES 4

SEASONED BROWN RICE

2 cups (440 g) uncooked brown rice
2 tablespoons oil
$^1/_4$ cup (30 g) shallots, thinly sliced
1–2 red finger-length chilies, deseeded and finely sliced
1 tablespoon peeled and finely grated fresh ginger
$3^1/_2$ cups (875 ml) stock or water
$^1/_2$ teaspoon salt

1 Put the rice in a bowl with enough cold water to cover. Gently rub the grains together with your fingers to remove any excess surface starch. Drain.
2 Place the oil in the rice cooker bowl, press "cook" and heat for 1 minute. Add the shallots, chilies and ginger and cook, stirring occasionally, until aromatic, 3–4 minutes. Add the rice and stir to coat the grains with the oil. Add the stock and salt.
3 Close the lid and press "cook." Cook until the rice cooker turns to "warm," 35–40 minutes. Fluff the rice with a rice paddle, close the lid and let stand for 10–15 minutes to absorb any remaining moisture.

SERVES 4

WILD RICE

Not a true rice, wild rice refers to the seeds of an aquatic grass. The longer the seeds, the more highly prized and the more expensive. The seeds are heated and partially hulled after harvest. This process and the length of the seeds affects the amount of water and the cooking time required. In general, wild rice takes longer to cook than conventional rice. Its unique nutty taste and chewy texture make it ideal for combining with other types of rice or with barley.

2 cups (440 g) uncooked wild rice
3 cups (750 ml) stock or water
$^1/_2$ teaspoon salt (optional)

SERVES 4

1 Combine the wild rice, stock and salt (if using) in the rice cooker bowl, spreading the rice evenly in the bottom of the bowl. Close the lid and press "cook." Cook until the cooker turns to "warm," about 40 minutes.
2 Fluff the rice with a rice paddle, close the lid and let stand for 10–15 minutes to absorb any remaining moisture.

Stir sautéed mushrooms, chopped garlic and chopped fresh thyme and fresh flat-leaf (Italian) parsley into the rice. Use as basis of a salad tossed with your favorite dressing and with nuts and fresh or dried fruit.

Right: Seasoned Brown Rice

CLASSIC SHRIMP FRIED RICE

2 cups (440 g) short-or medium-grain white rice
2 cups (500 ml) water
$^1/_4$ cup (45 g) dried lotus seeds (optional)
3 tablespoons oil
3 oz (90 g) spicy pork sausage, removed from casing and diced
6 dried black Chinese mushrooms, soaked until soft, rinsed well and squeezed dry, tough stems discarded, caps diced
1 carrot, peeled and diced
1 lb (500 g) medium shrimp, shelled, deveined and chopped, reserving 2 whole shrimp for garnish
1 small onion, diced
2 tablespoons fish sauce
$^1/_2$ teaspoon salt
Cracked peppercorns
$^1/_3$ cup (15 g) garlic (Chinese) chives, coarsely chopped
Fresh coriander (cilantro) sprigs, for garnish
1 red finger-length chili, deseeded and thinly sliced, for garnish

1 Put the rice in a bowl with enough cold water to cover. Gently rub the grains together with your fingers to remove any excess surface starch. Drain.

2 Combine the rice and water in the rice cooker bowl, spreading the rice evenly in the bottom of the bowl. Close the lid and press "cook." Cook until the rice cooker turns to "warm," 12–15 minutes. Transfer the rice to a bowl, cover and keep warm.

3 If using lotus seeds, soak in warm water to cover for 20 minutes. Insert a toothpick in the seeds from end to end to remove any bitter green sprouts. Cook the seeds in boiling water for 20 minutes. Drain.

4 Place half of the oil in the rice cooker bowl, press "cook" and heat for 1 minute. Working in batches, add the sausage, mushrooms, lotus seeds, carrot, shrimp and onion, and cook, stirring constantly, until the onion softens and the shrimp turn pink, about 5 minutes. Remove the whole shrimp and set aside for garnish. Stir in the fish sauce, salt, pepper to taste and all but 1 tablespoon of chopped chives.

5 Lightly oil a 2-qt (2-liter) bowl or eight 1-cup (250-ml) ramekins with the remaining 1$^1/_2$ tablespoons of oil. Fill the bowl or each ramekin one-third full with the cooked rice, pressing in place. Spread evenly with the sausage mixture, then cover with the remaining rice. Press to compact the layers firmly, then unmold onto a plate. If using a bowl, cut each remaining whole shrimp in half lengthwise. If using ramekins, cut each into 4 pieces. Garnish the rice with the shrimp, coriander sprigs and chili slices.

SERVES 6–8

MIXED RICE SALAD

1 cup (220 g) uncooked white rice, rinsed

1 cup (220 g) uncooked brown rice, rinsed

$1/_4$ cup (45 g) uncooked wild rice, rinsed

$3^1/_2$ cups (875 ml) chicken stock

1 small onion, halved and thinly sliced

$1^1/_2$ cups (375 g) drained oil-packed roasted bell peppers, finely sliced, or 1–2 fresh red bell peppers, roasted (see note), deseeded and finely sliced

6 oz (180 g) snowpeas (mange-tout), trimmed and thinly sliced on the diagonal

3 green onions (scallions), finely sliced

$1/_3$ cup (90 g) smoked almonds, coarsely chopped

DRESSING

$1/_4$ cup (60 ml) olive oil

3 tablespoons red wine vinegar

3 teaspoons soy sauce

1 teaspoon sesame oil

2 tablespoons bottled sweet chili sauce

1 Combine the rices and stock in the rice cooker bowl, spreading the rices evenly in the bottom of the bowl.

2 Close the lid and press "cook." Cook until the rice cooker turns to "warm," 35–40 minutes.

3 Meanwhile, make the Dressing by placing all the ingredients in a small bowl and whisk to combine.

4 Transfer the cooked rice to a bowl. Stir the Dressing through the rice and set aside to cool.

5 Add the onion, bell peppers, snowpeas, green onions and nuts, reserving a few for garnish, and toss to combine.

Add cooked shrimp, sliced smoked chicken or sliced, grilled, marinated beef.

To roast bell peppers—Put the peppers on a baking sheet in a hot oven (400°F/200°C). Turn occasionally, until the skin turns black and blistered. Transfer to a plate and tent with aluminum foil or put in a plastic bag. When the peppers are cool enough to handle, remove the blackened skin with paper towel, fingers or small paring knife. Remove the seeds and ribs.

SERVES 4–6

LEMON DILL RISOTTO

2 tablespoons oil

1 clove garlic, crushed

1 leek, sliced crosswise

1 1/2 cups (315 g) Arborio rice

1/2 cup (125 ml) dry white wine

2–3 cups (500–750 ml) vegetable or chicken stock

1/2 teaspoon salt

Cracked peppercorns

1/2 cup (60 g) grated Parmesan cheese

1–2 tablespoons lemon juice

1 teaspoon finely grated lemon rind

2 tablespoons chopped fresh dill

1 Place the oil in the rice cooker bowl, press "cook" and heat for 1 minute. Add the garlic and leek and cook, stirring constantly, until the leeks begin to soften, about 5 minutes.

2 Add the rice and stir to coat with the oil. Add the wine, stock, salt and pepper to taste.

3 Close the lid and press "cook." Cook until the cooker switches to "warm," 15–20 minutes, stirring halfway through the cooking time with a rice paddle.

4 Stir the rice, then fold in the cheese, lemon juice and rind. Close the lid and let stand for 10 minutes on "warm." Garnish with the dill before serving.

Cook diced chicken with the rice or add mixed seafood such as shrimp, mussels and calamari to the rice during the last 5 minutes of cooking.

SERVES 4

Other Grains

CINNAMON APPLE OATMEAL

1 cup (90 g) rolled oats
1¹/₂ cups (375 ml) apple or
   orange juice
³/₄ cup (180 ml) water
Pinch of salt (optional)
¹/₃ cup (60 g) mixed dried
   fruit such as golden
   raisins, chopped apples
   and chopped apricots
¹/₂ teaspoon ground cinnamon or nutmeg
¹/₂ cup (125 g) plain or fruit-
   flavored yogurt

SERVES 3–4

1 Combine the oats, fruit juice, water, salt (if using) and mixed dried fruit in the rice cooker bowl, spreading the ingredients evenly on the bottom of the bowl. Close the lid and press "cook."

2 Cook, stirring once halfway through cooking, until the oats and fruit are soft, 12–15 minutes. Let stand on "warm" with the lid closed for 10 minutes if a softer texture is desired.

3 Stir in the cinnamon and yogurt or serve the yogurt on side.

Substitute fresh fruit such as whole fresh berries or sliced peaches or bananas for the dried fruit.

BUTTERED MILLET

Millet has been a staple in Africa and Asia for centuries. The indigestible hull is removed from the round grains, making them cook fairly quickly and producing fluffy grains with a mild, delicate flavor. Millet benefits from being lightly toasted, with or without butter or oil. It combines well with other grains.

1 tablespoon unsalted butter

1 tablespoon oil

1 cup (180 g) millet, rinsed

2 cups (500 ml) stock or water

$^1/_2$ teaspoon salt

MAKES 2 cups (300 g)

1 Put the butter and oil in the rice cooker bowl and press "cook." When the butter is melted, add the millet and cook, stirring constantly, until toasted and golden, about 3 minutes.

2 Add the stock and salt. Close the lid and cook until the rice cooker switches to "warm," 25–30 minutes. Let stand for 5 minutes on "warm" with the lid closed before serving as a rice or oat substitute.

HEARTY BARLEY

1 cup (200 g) pearl barley, rinsed

2 cups (500 ml) stock or water

$^1/_2$ teaspoon salt

MAKES 2 cups (330 g)

1 Combine the barley, stock and salt in the rice cooker bowl, spreading the barley evenly over the bottom of the bowl.

2 Close the lid and press "cook." Cook until the rice cooker switches to "warm," about 35 minutes.

3 Fluff with a rice paddle, close the lid and let stand for 10 minutes to absorb any remaining liquid. Serve as a rice substitute.

Substitute half the stock or water with fruit juice and serve topped with fresh fruit.

BARLEY AND MUSHROOM RISOTTO WITH SPINACH

1 oz (30 g) dried porcini mushrooms
1 cup (250 ml) boiling water
1 tablespoon unsalted butter
1 tablespoon oil
1 large onion, chopped
1 clove garlic, crushed
1 cup (200 g) pearl barley
$^3/_4$ cup (180 ml) white wine
4 cups (1 liter) vegetable or chicken stock, plus more if
    needed
$^1/_2$ teaspoon salt
Cracked peppercorns
5 oz (150 g) fresh shiitake mushrooms, stems removed and
    caps sliced
1 cup (60 g) chopped fresh spinach
Grated rind and juice of 1 lemon
$^1/_2$ cup (60 g) grated Parmesan cheese

1 Soak the porcini mushrooms in a small bowl with
the boiling water for 30 minutes. Drain and chop.
2 Put the butter and oil in the rice cooker bowl and
press "cook." When the butter is melted, add the
onion and garlic and cook, stirring occasionally, until
the onion softens slightly, about 2 minutes.
3 Add the barley and stir to coat with the oil. Pour in
the wine and stir in the stock, salt and pepper to
taste. Close the lid and cook, stirring occasionally,
until the rice cooker switches to "warm," 55–60 minutes. Add more stock, close the lid and cook longer if
a softer texture is desired.
4 Stir in the porcini and shiitake mushrooms, spinach
and lemon rind and juice, close the lid and cook
until heated through, about 5 minutes. Serve, accompanied with the Parmesan cheese.

SERVES 3–4

TASTY HUMMUS DIP

1/4 lb (125 g) snowpeas
(mange-tout), trimmed
and blanched
12 thin asparagus spears,
ends trimmed, blanched
and cut into 3-in (7.5-cm)
lengths
1/4 lb (125 g) green beans,
trimmed and blanched
8–12 pieces pita bread

DIP
2 teaspoons cumin seeds
1 tablespoon oil plus 1/4
cup (60 ml)
1 onion, chopped
2 cloves garlic, crushed
1 cup (220 g) yellow split
peas, rinsed
1/4 cup (60 ml) lemon juice
1 red finger-length chili,
deseeded and finely
chopped (optional)
Salt and cracked pepper-
corns
1/2 cup (90 g) finely diced
red bell pepper
1/4 cup (10 g) chopped
fresh coriander leaves
(cilantro) or flat-leaf
(Italian) parsley

1 Make the Dip first by turning the rice cooker to "cook" and heat for 1 minute. Add the cumin seeds and toast, stirring constantly, until aromatic, about 2 minutes. Remove and set aside.

2 Add 1 tablespoon of the oil and heat for 1 minute. Add the onion and garlic and cook, stirring occasionally, until the onion softens slightly, 2–3 minutes. Add the split peas and enough water to cover them. Close the lid and press "cook." Cook until the peas are tender and beginning to break down, and the rice cooker switches to "warm," about 30 minutes. Drain and set aside to cool.

3 Puree the pea mixture in a food processor. With the motor running, gradually add the 1/4 cup (60 ml) of oil, then the lemon juice, cumin seeds, chili and salt and pepper to taste.

4 Transfer the Dip to a bowl and stir in the bell pepper and coriander leaves. Serve with the snowpeas, asparagus, green beans and pita bread.

Dip can also be served as an accompaniment to main meals.

SERVES 4–6

SPINACH AND YOGURT BEAN DIP

1 cup (220 g) dried can-
nellini beans, rinsed
About 3 cups (750 ml)
vegetable or chicken
stock or water
1 cup (220 g) chopped,
blanched spinach
3 tablespoons lime juice
2 cloves garlic, crushed
2 teaspoons ground cumin
1 cup (250 g) thick plain
yogurt
1/3 cup (60 g) chopped
drained oil-packed sun-
dried tomatoes
Salt and cracked pepper-
corns

SESAME TOASTS
4 pita breads, cut into
wedges
1 egg white, lightly beaten
1/3 cup (45 g) sesame
seeds
1/3 cup (45 g) grated
Parmesan cheese

1 Put the cannellini beans in the rice cooker bowl. Add enough stock to cover the beans. Close the lid and press "cook." Cook until the beans are tender, about 45 minutes. Drain and let cool.

2 Meanwhile, make the Sesame Toasts: Preheat the oven to 350°F (180°C). Arrange the pita wedges on a baking sheet and brush lightly with the egg white. Sprinkle half of the wedges with the sesame seeds and the other half with cheese. Bake until lightly browned and crisp, about 10 minutes. Toasts can be prepared ahead and stored in an airtight container for up to 1 week.

3 Puree the beans and spinach in a food processor. With the motor running, add the lime juice, garlic and cumin. Transfer the dip to a bowl and stir in the yogurt and tomatoes and season with the salt and pepper. Serve with the Sesame Toasts.

Canned cannellini beans can be used in this recipe. Do not cook the cannellini beans, simply rinse and puree.

SERVES 4–6

Pasta and Noodles

SHRIMP SOBA NOODLES

1¹/₂ lbs (750 g) medium
shrimp, peeled and
deveined
¹/₃ cup (90 ml) bottled
chili sauce
2¹/₂ cups (625 ml) hot
water or stock
10 oz (300 g) soba noo-
dles
2 teaspoons sesame oil
¹/₄ lb (125 g) snowpeas
(mange-tout), thinly
sliced on diagonal
1 red bell pepper, deseeded and thinly sliced
3 green onions (scallions),
thinly sliced
2 tablespoons chopped
fresh coriander leaves
(cilantro)
1 tablespoon sesame
seeds, toasted in a dry
skillet until golden

1 Toss the shrimp with half of the chili sauce in a
bowl.

2 Put the water or stock in the rice cooker bowl,
close the lid and press "cook." When the water comes
to a boil, add the shrimp, noodles, sesame oil and the
remaining chili sauce. Close the lid and cook until
most of the liquid is absorbed, about 4 minutes.

3 Stir in the snowpeas, bell pepper and green onions.
Close the lid and press "cook." Cook until the noodles are al dente, 1–2 minutes. Serve garnished with
the coriander leaves and sesame seeds.

Substitute sliced calamari, mussels in or out of shell or
other quick-cooking seafood for the shrimp. Seafood can
also be cooked in a steamer rack above the noodles.

SERVES 4

CHINESE CHICKEN NOODLE SOUP

1 whole chicken, 4–5 lbs
(2–2.5 kg)
1 onion, chopped
2 cloves garlic, crushed
2 bay leaves
8 cups (2 liters) chicken
stock
$3/4$ lb (440 g) fresh
hokkien noodles or other
$3/8$-in (1-cm) wide noo-
dles such as udon,
rinsed in warm water
1 cup (150 g) fresh or
frozen peas
2 carrots, peeled and thinly
sliced lengthwise
Salt and cracked pepper-
corns
2 tablespoons chopped
fresh flat-leaf (Italian)
parsley
Crusty bread, for serving

1 Cut the chicken into serving pieces: 2 half breasts, 2 thighs, 2 drumsticks and 2 wings, with the wing tips removed. Remove the skin from the chicken pieces and discard. Reserve the chicken back for another use.
2 Put the chicken pieces, onion, garlic, bay leaves and stock in the rice cooker bowl. Close the lid and press "cook." Bring to a boil and cook for 40 minutes.
3 Remove the chicken from the pot and pull the meat off the bones. Set aside and keep warm. Add the noodles, peas, carrots and chicken meat to the rice cooker bowl. Press "cook" and cook until heated through, about 5 minutes.
4 Remove the bay leaves and discard. Season with the salt and pepper. Serve garnished with the parsley and accompanied with crusty bread.

For a quick soup, rather than cook a whole chicken, purchase a barbecued chicken. Discard the skin, remove the
meat from the bones and shred, then stir into the liquid
with the vegetables.

SERVES 4

EASY TOMATO SAUCE PASTA

1 tablespoon oil

2 cloves garlic, crushed

1 red finger-length chili, deseeded and finely chopped
  (optional)

1 onion, chopped

$^3/_4$ lb (375 g) farfalle or fusilli

3 cups (750 ml) hot vegetable or chicken stock

1 can (14 oz/440 g) whole tomatoes

2 tablespoons tomato paste

2 tablespoons Worcestershire sauce

$^1/_2$ cup (20 g) chopped fresh basil

Salt and cracked peppercorns

$^1/_3$ cup (60 g) small pitted black olives such as Nicoise or
  Kalamata, sliced

1 Put the oil in the rice cooker bowl, press "cook"
and heat for 1 minute. Add the garlic, chili and onion
and cook, stirring occasionally, until the onion softens
slightly, about 2 minutes. Add the pasta, stock, tomatoes, tomato paste, Worcestershire sauce, half of the
basil, and salt and pepper to taste.

2 Close the lid and press "cook." Cook, stirring occasionally, until the pasta is al dente, about 10 minutes.
Stir in the olives, garnish with the remaining fresh
basil and serve.

Bringing liquid to a boil before adding pasta or noodles
helps prevent them sticking together. Alternatively, preheat
the liquid before pouring into the rice cooker bowl.

To make seafood pasta Steam mussels, peeled and
deveined shrimp, sliced calamari or a mixture of shellfish
in a steamer tray above the pasta according to cooking
time required. Serve on top of the cooked pasta or stir in
with the olives.

To make beef or chicken pasta Sauté ground beef or chicken
until brown. Add to the rice cooker with the pasta.

SERVES 4–6

COCONUT LAKSA CHICKEN SOUP

2 cups (500 ml) coconut
milk
$^1/_3$ cup (90 g) laksa paste
or Thai curry paste
2 cups (500 ml) chicken
stock
1 lb (500 g) skinless, boneless chicken breasts or
thighs, thinly sliced
2 tablespoons lime juice
$1^1/_2$ tablespoons fish
sauce
1 teaspoon shaved palm
sugar (optional)
1 lb (500 g) fresh rice noodles or hokkien noodles,
rinsed in hot water
$^1/_4$ lb (125 g) bean sprouts
$^1/_4$ cup (10 g) chopped
fresh coriander leaves
(cilantro)
$^1/_4$ cup (10 g) chopped
fresh mint

1 Put $^1/_2$ cup (125 ml) of the coconut milk and laksa paste in the rice cooker bowl and press "cook." Cook, stirring constantly, for 2 minutes.
2 Add the remaining coconut milk, chicken stock and sliced chicken. Close the lid and bring to a boil. Cook until the chicken is opaque, 5–10 minutes.
3 Stir in the lime juice and fish sauce. Taste and add the palm sugar, if using.
4 Divide the noodles into 4 large soup bowls, ladle over the hot coconut laksa soup with the sliced chicken. Garnish with the bean sprouts, coriander leaves and fresh mint.

Substitute 1 lb (500 g) shrimp, peeled and deveined for the chicken, or use $^1/_2$ lb (250 g) each chicken and shrimp.

If fresh rice noodles are not readily available, substitute $^1/_2$ lb (250 g) dried noodles. Pour boiling water over noo-dles and stand for 5 minutes or until soft. Drain.

SERVES 4

Meat Dishes

DELICIOUS CARAMELIZED PORK SPARERIBS

1 tablespoon oil

1¹/₂ lbs (750 g) beef or pork spareribs

¹/₂ cup (125 ml) hoisin sauce

³/₄ cup (180 ml) beef or chicken stock or water, plus more if needed

¹/₂ teaspoon Chinese five spice powder

1–2 red finger-length chilies, deseeded and thinly sliced (optional)

1 lb (500 g) baby potatoes

2 bunches asparagus spears, 6–7 oz (180–220 g) each, ends trimmed and spears cut in half

¹/₄ cup (10 g) chopped fresh coriander leaves (cilantro) or flat-leaf (Italian) parsley

2 green onions (scallions), thinly sliced

1 Place the oil in the rice cooker bowl, press "cook" and heat for 1 minute. Working in batches, cook the spareribs, turning occasionally, until browned, 5–6 minutes. Transfer to paper towels to drain.

2 Pour the oil from the rice cooker bowl. Return the bowl to the cooker and add the spareribs, hoisin sauce, stock, five spice powder, and chili (if using).

3 Close the lid and press "cook." Cook for 15 minutes, turning the ribs occasionally so they do not burn. Scatter the potatoes on top of the meat. Close the lid and cook for 10 minutes; carefully turning the meat and potatoes occasionally, so they brown evenly and do not burn.

4 Put the asparagus spears in a steamer tray and place above the meat, or lay the spears over the meat. Add more stock or water if needed. Close the lid and cook until the asparagus is tender but still firm, 3–5 minutes.

5 Remove the spareribs and vegetables from the cooker. Skim the oil from the cooking liquid and spoon the liquid over the spareribs. Garnish with coriander leaves and green onions.

SERVES 4

QUICK AND EASY TACOS

2 tablespoons oil
1 large onion, finely chopped
2 cloves garlic, crushed
1 red finger-length chili, deseeded and finely chopped
1 lb (500 g) ground beef or chicken
$^1/_2$ cup (125 ml) tomato paste
$^1/_2$ cup (125 ml) beef or chicken stock or water
2 tablespoons balsamic vinegar
1 can (14 oz/440 g) whole tomatoes with juice
1 teaspoon sugar
$^1/_2$ teaspoon salt
2 teaspoons paprika
2 teaspoons ground cumin
2 teaspoons ground coriander

FOR SERVING
12 taco shells or soft corn tortillas
$^1/_2$ head iceberg lettuce, shredded
2 tomatoes, finely diced
$^3/_4$ lb (375 g) cheddar cheese, grated
1 small avocado, peeled and diced

1 Place 1 tablespoon of the oil in the rice cooker bowl, press "cook" and heat for 1 minute. Add the onion, garlic and chili and cook until the onion softens slightly, about 3 minutes. Remove and set aside.
2 Add the remaining oil to the rice cooker bowl and, working in batches, cook the meat, stirring to break up any lumps, until browned, 5–6 minutes. Remove the meat and pour the oil from the bowl.
3 Return the bowl to the cooker and add the onion mixture, meat and the rest of the ingredients. Stir well to combine. Close the lid and press "cook." Cook, stirring occasionally, for 10 minutes.
4 Switch to "warm" and let stand until ready to transfer to a large bowl, or take the cooker directly to the table. Serve with the taco shells, lettuce, tomatoes, cheese and avocado, and let diners assemble their own tacos.

SERVES 4

BRAISED BEEF IN RED WINE SAUCE

2 cups (500 ml) dry red
  wine
2 cloves garlic, crushed
3/4 lb (375 g) beef fillet,
  cut in half lengthwise
1 tablespoon oil
1 1/2 cups (375 ml) beef
  stock or water
1 cup (220 g) dried can-
  nellini beans
3 large tomatoes or 1 can
  (14 oz/440 g) whole
  tomatoes
1 onion, cut into thin
  wedges
1 tablespoon balsamic
  vinegar
1 teaspoon salt

HORSERADISH CREAM
1 1/2 tablespoons prepared
  horseradish (wasabi)
1 cup (250 g) crème
  fraîche or thick plain
  yogurt
1–2 teaspoons lemon or
  lime juice
Salt, to taste

1 Combine 1/4 cup (60 ml) of the red wine and the garlic in a glass or ceramic bowl. Add the beef, turn to coat, cover and marinate at room temperature for 30 minutes.

2 Meanwhile, make the Horseradish Cream by stirring together all the ingredients in a bowl. Cover and set aside.

3 Drain the beef, reserving the marinade. Place the oil in the rice cooker bowl, press "cook" and heat for 2 minutes.

4 Add the beef and cook for 3–4 minutes on each side, or longer if well-done beef is desired. Remove and set aside.

5 Put the remaining red wine, reserved marinade, stock, beans, tomatoes, onion, vinegar and salt into the rice cooker bowl. Stir to combine, close the lid and press "cook." Cook, stirring occasionally, for 35 minutes.

6 Set the beef across the beans, close the lid and cook until the beans are tender, 5–10 minutes. Remove the beef, tent with aluminum foil and let stand for 5 minutes. Slice the beef across the grain. Serve on top of the beans, accompanied with the Horseradish Cream.

SERVES 4

BRAISED LAMB TENDERLOIN

1 lb (500 g) lamb tender-
loin, cut in half cross-
wise

2 teaspoons ground cumin

1 teaspoon ground
cinnamon

2 tablespoons ghee or oil

1 onion, cut into thin
wedges

2 cloves garlic, crushed

1/2 cup (60 g) dried chickpeas (garbanzo beans)

4 cups (1 liter) chicken or
vegetable stock, plus
more if needed

1 teaspoon salt

1 cup (220 g) uncooked
brown rice, rinsed

1/2 cup (90 g) mixed dried
fruit such as dark
raisins, golden raisins
and chopped apples

1/2 cup (90 g) whole pistachios or slivered almonds,
toasted

1/3 cup (90 g) thick plain
yogurt

1 tablespoon chopped
fresh mint

1 Rub the lamb with half of the cumin and cinnamon and set aside. Put 1 tablespoon of the ghee in
the rice cooker bowl, press "cook" and heat for 1
minute.

2 Add the onion and garlic and cook, stirring occasionally, until the onion softens slightly, about 2 minutes. Add the chickpeas, stock and salt. Close the lid
and cook for 10 minutes. Stir in the brown rice, fruit
and remaining cumin and cinnamon.

3 Close the lid and cook until the brown rice and
chickpeas are tender, about 35 minutes. If the rice
cooker turns to "warm," add more stock if needed
and press "cook." Transfer the brown rice mixture to
a serving bowl, cover and keep warm.

4 Wipe the rice cooker bowl with paper towels and
return the bowl to the cooker. Add the remaining
ghee, press "cook" and heat for 1 minute. Add the
lamb and cook for 3–4 minutes on each side, or
longer if the lamb is thick or if well-done lamb is
desired.

5 Remove, tent with aluminum foil and let stand
for 5 minutes. Slice the lamb across the grain. Serve
on top of the brown rice mixture, garnished with the
pistachios, a dollop of yogurt and chopped mint.

SERVES 4

Poultry Dishes

GLAZED CHINESE-STYLE DUCK

$^1/_2$ cup (125 ml) hoisin
  sauce
Grated rind and juice of 1
  orange
$^1/_2$ teaspoon Chinese five
  spice powder
1 red finger-length chili,
  deseeded and thinly
  sliced
4 duck breasts, about
  6 oz (180 g) each
1 teaspoon oil
$1^1/_2$ cups (375 ml) water
2 bunches choy sum, bok
  choy or other Asian green
  leafy vegetable, $1^1/_4$–$1^1/_2$
  lbs (625–750 g) total,
  trimmed and cut into
  short lengths
$^1/_4$ cup (10 g) chopped
  fresh coriander leaves
  (cilantro)
2 green onions (scallions),
  chopped
1 teaspoon sesame seeds,
  toasted in a dry skillet
  until golden

1 Stir together the hoisin sauce, orange rind and juice, five spice powder and chili in a glass or ceramic bowl. Add the duck breasts, turn to coat, cover and marinate, turning occasionally, for 30 minutes. Drain the duck, reserving the marinade.

2 Place the oil in the rice cooker bowl, press "cook" and heat for 1 minute. Working in batches if necessary, add the duck and cook until browned, 2–3 minutes. Remove the duck, pour the oil from the bowl and return the bowl to the cooker. Line a steamer tray with parchment (baking) paper. Put the duck and reserved marinade on the prepared steamer tray. Add the water to the cooker bowl, close the lid and press "cook."

3 When the water comes to a boil, place the steamer in the cooker. Close the lid and press "cook." Cook until the duck is tender and the juices run clear when a knife is inserted into the thickest part away from the bone, 20–25 minutes.

4 Remove the duck, tent with aluminum foil and keep warm. Press "cook" and add more water to the cooker bowl if necessary. When the water is boiling, add the greens and cook until wilted, about 2 minutes. Serve the duck on the greens, garnished with the coriander leaves, green onions and sesame seeds.

SERVES 4

MISO SOUP WITH DUMPLINGS

8 cups (2 liters) water

$3/4$ cup (180 ml) soy sauce

$2/3$ cup (150 ml) mirin or
    sake

1 tablespoon sugar

1 lb (500 g) ground chicken

1 tablespoon shiro miso

1 egg, lightly beaten

2 tablespoons all-purpose
    (plain) flour

1–2 tablespoons pickled
    ginger, chopped, plus
    pickled ginger, for
    garnish

3 green onions (scallions),
    finely shredded

1 tablespoon sesame
    seeds, toasted in a dry
    skillet until golden

SERVES 4–6

1 Put the water, soy sauce, mirin or sake, and sugar in the rice cooker. Close the lid, press "cook" and bring to a simmer.

2 Stir together the chicken, miso, egg, flour and chopped pickled ginger in a bowl. Using 2 spoons or dampened hands, shape the chicken mixture into 1-in (2.5-cm) balls.

3 Place the balls in the simmering liquid. Stir once to make sure the balls are not sticking together. Close the lid, press "cook" and cook until a dumpling is no longer pink in the center, about 5 minutes. Cook in 2 batches if using a small rice cooker. Serve in bowls, garnished with the pickled ginger, green onions and sesame seeds.

Dumplings can be served hot or cold as finger food, accompanied by sweet chili sauce or plum dipping sauce.

To make chicken dumplings and rice. Remove the cooked dumplings from the rice cooker and keep warm. Remove half of the soup (refrigerate or freeze and use in another soup or in a sauce). Combine 3 tablespoons corn-starch with $1/3$ cup (90 ml) water and stir into the hot liquid. Cook, uncovered, over low heat until a thick, clear sauce forms. Serve with steamed rice and pickled ginger.

MARSALA SAUCE CHICKEN

1 tablespoon oil
1 clove garlic, crushed
1 teaspoon peeled and
 grated fresh ginger
1 leek or onion, diced
1¹/₂ lbs (750 g) boneless,
 skinless chicken thighs,
 cut into 1-in (2.5-cm)
 cubes
¹/₂ cup (125 ml) chicken
 stock
¹/₂ cup (125 ml) marsala
1 teaspoon Chinese five
 spice powder or allspice
1 tablespoon balsamic
 vinegar
¹/₂ red bell pepper,
 deseeded and diced
1 large mango, peeled and
 pitted, then cut into 1-in
 (2.5-cm) cubes
2 tablespoons cornstarch
 dissolved in ¹/₄ cup (60
 ml) water
Rice (pages 20–21) or
 potatoes (page 10), for
 serving
¹/₄ cup (45 g) hazelnuts,
 toasted and coarsely
 chopped

1 Place the oil in the rice cooker bowl, press "cook" and heat for 1 minute. Add the garlic, ginger and leek and cook, stirring occasionally, until the leeks soften slightly, 3–4 minutes.

2 Add the chicken, stock, marsala, five spice powder and vinegar. Close the lid and cook for 12 minutes.

3 Stir in the bell pepper and mango, then the cornstarch mixture. Press "cook" and cook, uncovered, until the sauce thickens and the chicken is opaque, about 5 minutes. Serve with potatoes or rice, garnished with the hazelnuts.

If you have a steamer tray, place the baby or diced potatoes on the tray and set above the chicken to cook for 10–15 minutes, depending on size. Brown the potatoes in the rice cooker before cooking the chicken.

To toast the hazelnuts, place the nuts in a baking pan and toast at 350°F (180° C) until fragrant and beginning to change color, 10–15 minutes. When the nuts are cool enough to handle, place in a kitchen towel and rub gently to remove most of the skins.

SERVES 4

ROSEMARY CHICKEN WITH MASHED POTATOES

4 skinless, boneless chicken breast halves, 6–7 oz (180–200 g) each

1 tablespoon soy sauce

1 tablespoon oil

Parchment (baking) paper or aluminum foil

1 large leek, sliced cross-wise

2 teaspoons unsalted butter, cut into 4 pieces

$1/3$ cup (90 ml) dry white wine

1 cup (180 g) Greek-style green olives, pitted and chopped

$1/4$ cup (10 g) fresh rosemary leaves

$1^1/2$ cups (375 ml) chicken stock

$1^1/4$ lbs (600 g) potatoes such as Desiree or Yukon gold, peeled and cut into 2-in (5-cm) pieces

2–3 tablespoons unsalted butter or $1/2$ cup (125 ml) heavy cream

2 tablespoons salted small capers, rinsed and drained

SERVES 4

1 Place the chicken in a bowl, drizzle with the soy sauce and turn to coat.

2 Put the oil in the rice cooker bowl, press "cook" and heat for 1 minute. Working in batches, add the chicken and cook until browned, about 5 minutes.

3 Cut four 12-in (30-cm) squares of parchment (baking) paper or aluminum foil. Place the leeks in the center, dividing evenly. Put a chicken breast on top of the leeks. Top each with a piece of butter. Evenly drizzle with the wine and top with olives and rosemary.

4 Bring 2 opposite sides of the paper over the chicken and fold twice to seal. Twist the ends of the parcel to close securely.

5 Pour the stock into the rice cooker bowl. Place the parcels on a steamer tray (or on a plate on top of a trivet) over the stock. Close the lid, press "cook" and cook for 10 minutes. Remove the steamer tray and add the potatoes to the stock.

6 Return the tray to the cooker. Cook until the juices run clear when a knife is inserted in the thickest part of the chicken breast and the potatoes are tender, about 15 minutes. Transfer the potatoes to a bowl and mash. Stir in the butter and capers. Serve the chicken and leeks on top of the mashed potatoes, drizzled with the juices in each parcel.

Before cooking the chicken, cut a horizontal pocket in each chicken breast, fill with the herbs, leeks and olives and seal with 1 or 2 toothpicks.

HONEY SOY CHICKEN

3 tablespoons soy sauce
1 tablespoon honey
1 teaspoon sesame oil
1 teaspoon peeled and
  grated fresh ginger
1/4 teaspoon ground star
  anise or cinnamon
12 drumsticks or 4 whole
  legs, about 3 lbs (1.5 kg)
  total
1 tablespoon oil
3/4 cup (180 ml) chicken
  stock
1 tablespoon cornstarch
  dissolved in 2 table-
  spoons water (optional)

COUSCOUS
1¹/₂ cups (280 g) instant
  couscous
1¹/₂ cups (375 ml) orange
  juice
2 teaspoons grated
  orange rind
1–2 tablespoons butter,
  melted
1/4 cup (10 g) chopped
  fresh flat-leaf (Italian)
  parsley
1/4 cup (45 g) macadamia
  nuts, toasted and
  coarsely chopped

1 Stir together the soy sauce, honey, sesame oil, ginger and star anise powder in a glass or ceramic bowl.
2 Add the chicken pieces, turn to coat, cover and marinate, turning occasionally, for at least 30 minutes.
3 Place the oil in the rice cooker bowl, press "cook" and heat for 1 minute.
4 Drain the chicken, reserving the marinade. Working in batches, cook the chicken pieces until lightly browned, about 5 minutes. Remove and set aside.
5 Pour off the fat and wipe the rice cooker bowl with paper towels. Return the bowl to the rice cooker and add the chicken, stock and reserved marinade. Close the lid, press "cook" and cook, turning occasionally, until the chicken is opaque, 20–30 minutes, depending on thickness.
6 Meanwhile, make the Couscous. Place the couscous in a heatproof bowl. Bring the orange juice to a boil in a saucepan over medium-high heat. Pour over the couscous and let stand for 5 minutes. Fluff with a fork and stir in the grated orange rind, melted butter, parsley and nuts.
7 Serve the chicken on top of the couscous, and drizzle with the cooking liquid. Alternatively, remove the chicken meat from the bones, stir into the cooking liquid and serve over the couscous. If a thicker sauce is desired, remove the chicken and add the cornstarch mixture to the cooking liquid. Cook, uncovered, over low heat until thickened.

SERVES 4

Seafood Dishes

STEAMED MUSSELS WITH WINE

1 tablespoon oil
2 cloves garlic, crushed
1 red finger-length chili, deseeded and finely chopped
(optional)
2 large tomatoes, chopped
2 lbs (1 kg) mussels, scrubbed and debearded
$1/2$ cup (125 ml) dry red wine
1–2 tablespoons red wine vinegar
$1/2$ teaspoon salt
$1/4$ cup (10 g) chopped fresh flat-leaf (Italian) parsley
$1/4$ cup (10 g) chopped fresh basil
3 green onions (scallions), chopped

1 Place the oil in the rice cooker bowl, press "cook" and heat for 1 minute. Add the garlic and chili (if using) and cook, stirring frequently, until aromatic, about 2 minutes.
2 Add the tomatoes and cook for 2 minutes. Add the mussels (discarding any that do not close to the touch), wine, vinegar and salt. Close the lid and cook, stirring occasionally, for about 8 minutes until the mussels open. Discard any mussels that do not open.
3 Stir in the parsley, basil and green onions, reserving some for garnish.

Cook $3/4$ lb (375 g) angel hair pasta in lightly salted water. Drain and toss with 1–2 tablespoons extra-virgin olive oil. Serve the mussels on the pasta, or toss the mussels with the pasta.

SERVES 4

TERIYAKI SHRIMP NOODLES

1/4 cup (60 ml) teriyaki sauce
1/4 cup (60 ml) bottled sweet chili sauce
2 lbs (1 kg) medium shrimp, peeled and deveined, tails intact
2 tablespoons oil
2 bunches asparagus spears, 6–7 oz (180–220 g) each, ends trimmed and spears cut on diagonal into 1-in (2.5-cm) pieces
1 lb (500 g) fresh hokkien or udon noodles, rinsed in hot water
1/3 cup (15 g) chopped garlic (Chinese) chives

1 Stir together the teriyaki and chili sauces in a glass or ceramic bowl. Add the shrimp, stir to coat, cover and marinate for 15 minutes.
2 Place the oil in the rice cooker bowl, press "cook" and heat for 2–3 minutes.
3 Drain the shrimp, reserving the marinade. Add the shrimp and asparagus to the rice cooker bowl. Close the lid and cook, stirring twice, until the shrimp start to turn bright pink, 3–4 minutes.
4 Add the reserved marinade and noodles. Cook until heated through, 2–3 minutes. Garnish with the chives.

SERVES 4

GARLIC AND CHILI SHRIMP

3 tablespoons oil
2 lbs (1 kg) uncooked medium shrimp, peeled and deveined, tails intact
2 red finger-length chilies, deseeded and thinly sliced
4 cloves garlic, thinly sliced
1/3 cup (15 g) chopped fresh flat-leaf (Italian) parsley or fresh coriander leaves (cilantro)

1 Place the oil in the rice cooker bowl, press "cook" and heat for 2–3 minutes.
2 Add the shrimp, chilies and garlic. Close the lid and cook, stirring twice, until the shrimp turn bright pink, 4–5 minutes. Garnish with the parsley.

Serve hot or cold with mixed green salad and crusty bread or toss with cooked pasta or rice.

SERVES 4

Left: Teriyaki Shrimp Noodles

SEAFOOD WONTON DUMPLINGS

2 teaspoons peeled and
  grated fresh ginger
1 tablespoon soy sauce
1 tablespoon Chinese rice
  wine or sake
1 teaspoon sesame oil
16 sea scallops or jumbo
  shrimp
16 round wonton wrappers
2 green onions (scallions),
  finely chopped
3 oz (90 g) snowpeas
  (mange-tout), finely
  chopped
8 cups (2 liters) water
Bottled sweet chili sauce
  or plum sauce, for
  serving

SERVES 4

1 Stir together the ginger, soy sauce, wine and oil in a glass or ceramic bowl. Add the scallops or jumbo shrimp, turn to coat well, cover and marinate for 15 minutes.

2 Place the wonton wrappers on a clean work surface and cover with a damp kitchen towel. Working with 1 wrapper at a time, place 1 scallop or shrimp and some green onions and snowpeas in the center of the wrapper. Lightly brush the edge of half of the wrapper with water. Fold the brushed side over the dry side. Beginning at one end, gently press the edges to seal and force out any excess air (excess air can cause the wrapper to burst open during cooking). Set aside and cover with a damp kitchen towel. Repeat with the remaining wrappers.

3 Put the water in the rice cooker bowl, close the lid and press "cook." When the water comes to a boil, add the dumplings. Gently stir to prevent the dumplings from sticking together. Close the lid and cook until the dumplings float to the surface and the wonton wrappers are soft and translucent, 3–4 minutes. Remove with a slotted spoon. Serve with a drizzle of the plum or sweet chili sauce.

To steam the dumplings, put the water in the rice cooker, close the lid and press "cook." Line a steamer tray with parchment (baking) paper and arrange the dumplings on the prepared tray (leaving space around the edges for the steam to circulate). When the water comes to a boil, put the tray over the water. Close the lid and cook until the wonton wrappers are soft and translucent, 5–6 minutes.

To make ginger-scallop soup, cook the dumplings in fish or chicken stock. Serve the soup and dumplings garnished with green onions. Serve the sauces on the side.

STEAMED FISH FILLETS

$^1/_4$ cup (60 ml) soy sauce

2 tablespoons lime or
lemon juice

1 tablespoon grated lime
or lemon rind

4 green onions (scallions),
chopped

1 tablespoon peeled and
grated fresh ginger

1 clove garlic, crushed

1 red finger-length chili,
deseeded and finely
chopped (optional)

4 kaffir lime leaves, center
rib removed and finely
sliced

Parchment (baking) paper
and aluminum foil

4 fish fillets or steaks,
such as salmon, about
6 oz (180 g) each

2 mangoes, peeled, pitted,
and sliced

1 cup (250 ml) water

1 recipe Seasoned Brown
Rice (page 30)

SERVES 4

1 Stir together the soy sauce, lime juice and rind, green onions, ginger, garlic, chili (if using) and kaffir lime leaves in a bowl.

2 Cut four 12-in (30-cm) squares of parchment (baking) paper. Place a fillet or steak in the center of each square. Place the lime mixture and mango on top of the fish, dividing evenly.

3 Bring 2 opposite sides of the paper over the fish and fold twice to seal. Twist the ends of the parcel to close securely. Wrap each parcel in a 12-in (30-cm) square of aluminum foil.

4 Pour the water into the rice cooker bowl. Place the fish parcels on a steamer tray (or on a plate on top of a trivet) over the water, press "cook", close the lid and cook for 8–10 minutes, depending on the thickness of the fillets. Serve with the Seasoned Brown Rice.

Substitute kaffir lime leaves with lemongrass. Use only the inner part of the thick bulb of the stem (the bottom one-third of the stem). Slice or bruise the lemongrass by gently hitting it with a meat mallet or the handle of a knife.

Substitute mango with peach.

SCRAMBLED EGGS WITH SMOKED SALMON

2 tablespoons crème
  fraîche or thick plain
  yogurt
2 teaspoons lemon juice
1 teaspoon unsalted butter
1 teaspoon oil
2 green onions (scallions),
  finely sliced
1/4 cup (45 g) finely diced
  red bell pepper
1 cup (60 g) shredded
  spinach
4 large eggs, lightly beaten
1/4 cup (60 ml) milk or half
  milk and heavy cream
2 tablespoons chopped fresh
  flat-leaf (Italian) parsley
  or chives (optional)
Salt and cracked pepper-
  corns
4 slices smoked salmon,
  cut into strips 3/4-in
  (2-cm) wide
2 sprigs fresh dill, for
  garnish
2 slices whole-grain bread,
  toasted

1 Stir together the crème fraîche or yogurt and lemon juice in a bowl. Set aside.

2 Place the butter and oil in the rice cooker bowl, press "cook" and heat for 1 minute.

3 When the butter is melted, add the green onions, bell pepper and spinach and cook, stirring occasionally, until the spinach is wilted, about 2 minutes.

4 Stir together the eggs, milk, and parsley (if using) in a bowl, and season with the salt and pepper.

5 Pour into the rice cooker bowl and gently stir until just cooked, 3–4 minutes. Serve topped with the smoked salmon, lemon crème and dill. Accompany with toasted bread.

Other ingredients, such as diced ham, diced tomato, diced celery, fresh corn kernels and/or pesto, can be used to flavor the eggs.

SERVES 2

Vegetable Dishes

CLASSIC POTATO GRATIN

1 tablespoon oil
1 onion, sliced
1 lb (500 g) potatoes such as Desiree or Yukon gold
1 large sweet potato (kumera), about $^3/_4$ lb (375 g),
   peeled and thinly sliced
$^3/_4$ cup (90 g) grated Gruyère or Parmesan cheese
$1^1/_2$ cups (375 ml) vegetable or chicken stock or water
$^1/_2$ cup (125 ml) heavy cream

1 Place the oil in the rice cooker bowl, press "cook" and heat for 1 minute. Add the onion and cook, stirring occasionally, until the onion softens slightly, about 2 minutes. Remove the onion. Layer one-third of the potatoes, sweet potatoes and the onion in the bottom of the rice cooker bowl.

2 Sprinkle with one-third of the cheese, reserving 1 tablespoon for the top. Continue making the layers, finishing with sprinkling of the cheese.

3 Pour in the stock. Close the lid, press "cook" and cook until the potatoes are soft when a knife is inserted in the center of the gratin, 35–40 minutes. Pour in the cream.

4 Close the lid, press "cook" and cook for 5 minutes. Turn to "warm" and let stand for 10 minutes. If desired, invert a heatproof plate over the rice cooker bowl and invert the plate and bowl together to unmold the gratin.

5 Place under a preheated broiler (grill) and broil (grill) until the top is golden.

Substitute pumpkin for some of the potato if desired.

SERVES 4–6

THAI VEGETARIAN CURRY

1 tablespoon oil

1 large onion, cut into
wedges

1 clove garlic, crushed

$1/4$ cup (60 ml) Massaman
curry paste

$3/4$ lb (375 g) round Thai
eggplants, tops removed
and quartered, or long
Asian eggplants, diced

1 lb (500 g) butternut or
other winter squash
(pumpkin), peeled and
cut into 1-in (2.5-cm)
cubes

1 cup (220 g) dried red
lentils, rinsed

3 cups (750 ml) vegetable
stock, or more if needed

2 teaspoons fish sauce

2 teaspoons sugar (optional)

1 cup (155 g) fresh or frozen
peas or green beans

2 kaffir lime leaves, center
rib removed and finely
sliced

2 tablespoons chopped
fresh coriander leaves
(cilantro), optional

1 Add the oil to the rice cooker bowl, press "cook" and heat for 1 minute. Add the onion and garlic and cook, stirring occasionally, until the onion softens slightly, 2 minutes.

2 Stir in the curry paste and cook for 2 minutes. Add the eggplants, squash, lentils, stock, fish sauce and sugar (if using).

3 Close the lid, press "cook" and cook until the squash is tender when a knife is inserted, about 20 minutes.

4 Stir in the peas and cook for 5 minutes, adding more stock if needed. Garnish with the kaffir lime leaves and coriander leaves (if using) and serve with rice.

Sauté diced firm tofu and cook with the curry. Or place peeled and deveined shrimp in a steamer basket over the curry and cook until bright pink, about 5 minutes. Serve the shrimp on top of the curry or carefully fold into the curry. Stir 1 cup (250 ml) coconut cream into the curry for a creamier texture and flavor.

SERVES 4

FRESH ASPARAGUS WITH PARMESAN

2 tablespoons oil
1 tablespoon balsamic
  vinegar
Pinch of salt
2 cups (500 ml) water
2 bunches asparagus
  spears, 6–7 oz (180–
  220 g) each, ends trimmed
1/3 cup (45 g) grated
  Parmesan cheese
Cracked peppercorns

SERVES 4

1 Whisk together the oil, vinegar and salt in a small bowl. Set aside.
2 Put the water in the rice cooker bowl. Close the lid and press "cook." When the water comes to a boil, add the asparagus.
3 Close the lid and cook until tender, 2–4 minutes, depending on the thickness. Drain, transfer to a warmed bowl and drizzle with the vinegar mixture. Sprinkle with Parmesan and season with pepper.

Asparagus can also be cooked in a steamer tray placed over the simmering water in the rice cooker bowl for 3–5 minutes, depending on the thickness.

BABY POTATOES WITH LEMON PEPPER

16 baby potatoes, about 3
  lbs (1.5 kg) total
6 cups (1.5 liters) water or
  vegetable or chicken
  stock
1–2 tablespoons unsalted
  butter
1 teaspoon cracked pep-
  percorns
1/2–1 teaspoon grated
  lemon rind

SERVES 4

1 Put the potatoes and water in the rice cooker bowl. Close the lid, press "cook" and cook until tender, about 10 minutes. Remove the potatoes and discard the water.
2 Return the rice bowl to the cooker and add the potatoes, butter, pepper and lemon rind, turning the potatoes to coat with the butter and seasonings. If desired, let stand on "warm" until serving.

If cooking potatoes in the stock, reserve the stock and use for soups or sauces.

Left: Fresh Asparagus with Parmesan

PERFECT CORN ON THE COB

2 tablespoons bottled
sweet chili sauce
2 tablespoons finely
chopped fresh coriander
leaves (cilantro) or flat-
leaf (Italian) parsley
1 teaspoon sesame oil
Pinch of salt
4 ears of corn, husks
removed
Parchment (baking) paper
or aluminum foil
2 cups (500 ml) hot water

SERVES 4

1 Stir together the chili sauce, coriander leaves, sesame oil and salt in a small bowl.

2 Put the corn in a shallow dish and drizzle with the chili sauce mixture, turning to coat well.

3 Cut four 12-in (30-cm) squares of parchment (baking) paper or aluminum foil. Place 1 ear of corn in the center of each square.

4 Bring 2 opposite sides of the paper over the corn and fold twice to seal. Twist the ends of the parcel to close securely.

5 Place on a steamer tray. Pour the hot water into the rice cooker bowl. Press "cook" and bring to a boil. Place the steamer tray over the water, close the lid and cook until the corn is tender, about 10 minutes.

To cook parcels without using the steamer tray, wrap each parcel in a 12-in (30-cm) square of aluminum foil. Pour the water into the rice cooker bowl and set the parcels in the water. Cooking time will be slightly shorter.

CARAMELIZED SWEET POTATOES

4 cups (1 liter) water
1¹/₂ lbs (750 g) sweet potatoes (kumeras), peeled
and cut into 1¹/₂-in (4-cm)
pieces
Pinch of salt
¹/₄ cup (60 ml) pure maple
syrup
¹/₂ teaspoon ground cinnamon
2 teaspoons sesame
seeds, toasted in a dry
skillet until golden

1 Put the water, sweet potatoes and salt in the rice cooker bowl. Close the lid, press "cook" and cook until just tender, about 10 minutes. Remove the potatoes with slotted spoon. Discard the water.

2 Return the bowl to the cooker and add the potatoes, maple syrup and cinnamon. Press "cook," close the lid and cook, turning once, until caramelized, 5–10 minutes. Serve sprinkled with the sesame seeds.

SERVES 4

Right: Perfect Corn on the Cob

Desserts

SWEET RICE PUDDING

1¹/₂ cups (315 g) short-or medium-grain white rice, rinsed
1 cup (250 ml) water
1 cup (250 ml) apple or black currant juice
¹/₂ teaspoon ground cinnamon
¹/₄ teaspoon salt
1 cup (125 g) blueberries or strawberries
1 tablespoon lime or lemon juice
1 teaspoon grated lime or lemon rind
¹/₂ cup (60 g) berry yogurt
¹/₃ cup (60 g) hazelnuts, toasted (page 65) and coarsely
   chopped

1 Put the rice, water, fruit juice, cinnamon and salt in the rice cooker bowl and stir to combine. Close the lid and press "cook."
2 Cook, stirring once, until the rice cooker turns to "warm," about 15 minutes.
3 Stir the rice with a rice paddle, then fold in the blueberries or strawberries, lime or lemon juice and rind and yogurt. Close the lid and let stand for 10 minutes on "warm." Sprinkle with the hazelnuts.

To make Blueberry Rice Brûlé, divide the blueberry rice among ramekins and refrigerate. Sprinkle a thin layer of brown or Demerara sugar over the rice in each ramekin. Place the ramekins in the preheated broiler (grill) until the sugar turns golden, 3–4 minutes, being careful that the sugar does not burn.

SERVES 4

QUICK FRUIT CAKE FLAN

CRUST

12 ginger cookies, about
    6 oz (180 g) total
¹/₂ cup (60 g) walnuts
1 teaspoon ground cinna-
    mon or nutmeg
5 tablespoon (²/₃ stick/
    70 g) unsalted butter,
    melted

FILLING

1 lb (500 g) rhubarb, cut in-
    to ³/₄-in (2-cm) pieces
2 pears such as Bartlett or
    Comice, quartered
    lengthwise, cores
    removed and cut into
    slices ¹/₄ in (6 mm) wide
³/₄ cup (180 g) sugar
³/₄ cup (180 ml) water
1 tablespoon lime or lemon
    juice
2 teaspoons grated lime or
    lemon rind
1 teaspoon soy sauce
3 tablespoons cornstarch
    dissolved in ¹/₄ cup
    (60 ml) water
1 cup (125 g) fresh or
    frozen blueberries or
    other berries

1 To make the Crust, place the cookies in a plastic bag and, using a meat mallet or rolling pin, crush until the cookies are fine crumbs. (Using a food processor may strain the motor.)

2 Place the walnuts in another plastic bag and crush. Combine the cookie crumbs, crushed walnuts and cinnamon in a bowl. Stir in the melted butter.

3 Remove the sides from an 8-in (20-cm) springform pan. Place a sheet of parchment (baking) paper over the pan bottom and replace the sides. Do not trim the sheet but allow to protrude from the pan. Place the crust mixture in the pan and, using a flat-bottomed glass, press until evenly spread and firm. Refrigerate until needed.

4 To make the Filling, put the rhubarb, pears, sugar, water, juice, rind and soy sauce in the rice cooker bowl.

5 Close the lid, press "cook" and cook, stirring twice, until the rhubarb starts to soften, 5–6 minutes. Gently stir the cornstarch mixture and blueberries into the rhubarb.

6 Cook uncovered, stirring, until the fruit thickens. Remove the bowl from the rice cooker and let the Filling cool but not set. Pour into the springform pan over the chilled crust. Refrigerate until set and chilled, 30 minutes.

If the rhubarb is very juicy, add 2 tablespoons extra cornstarch to help the mixture stiffen and set.

SERVES 6–8

PEACHES POACHED IN CINNAMON WINE SAUCE

$^1/_2$ cup (45 g) flaked coconut
$^1/_2$ cup (60 g) pecans, coarsely chopped
2–3 teaspoons unsalted butter
4 large peaches, 2 lbs (1 kg) total, halved and pitted
$^1/_2$ cup (125 ml) tawny port
$^1/_2$ cup (125 g) thick plain yogurt
1 tablespoon honey
$^1/_4$ teaspoon ground allspice or cinnamon

1 Put the flaked coconut and pecans in the rice cooker bowl. Press "cook" and cook, stirring constantly, until the coconut is golden, 3–4 minutes. Transfer to a plate.
2 Wipe the bowl with paper towels and return to the cooker. Put the butter in the rice cooker bowl and press "cook." When the butter is melted, working in batches, add the peach halves, cut side down, and cook until golden, 2–3 minutes.
3 Using plastic tongs, carefully remove the peaches. Add the port to the rice cooker bowl and stir to release any cooked bits from the bottom of the bowl. Return the peaches to the rice cooker bowl, cut side up. Close the lid and cook, turning once, until the peaches are just beginning to soften, 6–8 minutes. Remove the peaches.
4 Press "cook" and cook the liquid, uncovered, until thickened, about 2 minutes. Stir together the yogurt and honey in a bowl. Put 2 peach halves on each plate. Top with the honey yogurt and garnish with the coconut and pecans. Drizzle the sauce around peaches.

Other fruits, such as nectarines, apricots and mango may be used in place of the peaches. Substitute toasted hazelnuts or macadamias for the pecans, and stir the nuts and coconut into the yogurt just before serving.

SERVES 4

BLACK RICE PUDDING WITH COCONUT CREAM

1¹/₂ cups (315 g) uncooked Thai black rice, rinsed
2¹/₂ cups (625 ml) water
¹/₂ teaspoon salt
1 mango
¹/₄ cup (45 g) shaved palm sugar or brown sugar
¹/₂ cup (125 ml) coconut cream
2 teaspoons sesame seeds, toasted in a dry skillet until golden

SERVES 4

1 Put the rice in a bowl with enough water to cover and let stand overnight. Drain and put the rice, water and salt in the rice cooker bowl, spreading the rice evenly in the bottom of the bowl.
2 Close the lid and press "cook." Cook until the rice cooker turns to "warm," about 40 minutes.
3 Prepare the mango by cutting the flesh away from each side of the pit. Peel each half and chop the flesh.
4 Stir the chopped mango and sugar into the cooked rice. Close the lid and let stand until heated through, 5–10 minutes. Swirl the coconut cream through the cooked rice and garnish with the sesame seeds.

This rice pudding can also be served chilled.

CRANBERRY ORANGE RICE PUDDING

1¹/₂ cups (375 ml) water
1¹/₄ cups (265 g) uncooked long-grain white rice, rinsed
1 cup (125 g) fresh or dried cranberries
1 cup (250 ml) orange juice
Grated rind of 1 orange
¹/₂ teaspoon ground cinnamon
¹/₄ teaspoon salt
1 cup (125 g) pecans, toasted and coarsely chopped

1 Combine the water, rice, cranberries, orange juice and rind, cinnamon and salt in the rice cooker bowl, spreading the rice evenly in the bottom of the bowl. Close the lid and press "cook."
2 Cook, stirring occasionally, until the rice cooker turns to "warm," 12–15 minutes. Serve garnished with the chopped pecans.

For a more impressive presentation, serve the rice in hollowed out orange rinds. After juicing the oranges, reserve the orange rinds. Remove any orange flesh and spoon the cranberry rice into the rinds to serve.

SERVES 4

Left: Black Rice Pudding with Coconut Cream

INDEX